THE BIG BOOK OF
CATS

EDITED BY J.C. SUARÈS

welcome
BOOKS

NEW YORK SAN FRANCISCO

F O R E W O R D

THIS IS MY TWENTIETH BOOK ABOUT CATS. I've either edited, designed, written, or illustrated one almost every year since *The Illustrated Cat*, which came out in the seventies. You'd think that I could probably answer any question about cats after all this time, but they remain a mystery. Sure, I can tell the difference between a Persian and a Siamese and a Himalayan, and I know that calicos are always female. But how does purring work? Do cats dream? Does it really help to have an "s" sound in their name? (Sam vs. Myron?) And why do they play with their dead victims? One thing is sure, however: I've got a list of my favorite cats of all time. It includes real cats and fictitious ones.

No. 1: Morris the Cat

My all-time hero. The large, orange TV spokesman for 9-lives cat food, called Lucky before his rise to fame, was "discovered" at the Human Society of Hingdale, Illinois. With his macho looks and cool demeanor, he was so good at selling 9-Lives that he was made an honorary director of the parent company, Star Kist Foods, Inc., and given power to reject new cat-food flavors. When he passed away in 1978, it made the evening news.

FOREWORD

Morris's official biographer, Barbara Burn (*Morris: An Intimate Biography*), said, "This cat really was special…thirty-nine out of forty people on the street recognized him, and that, I think, is amazing."

An intense two-and-a-half-year search for a suitable successor resulted in a lookalike—another stray, of course—this one found in California.

NO. 2: ORANGEY

If Morris ruled television, Orangey was, for a while, the busiest cat in the movies. He appeared with Ray Milland in *Rhubarb*, Jackie Gleason in *Gigot*, and Audrey Hepburn in *Breakfast at Tiffany's*. He stole most of the scenes he was in and won two Patsys, the Oscar of the animal entertainment world.

Orangey was a cantankerous prima donna, disliked even by his trainer, Frank Inn. However, he was a survivor and a genuine talent who "could play any part," according to Inn.

NO. 3: THE CHESHIRE CAT

"The cat only grinned when it saw Alice," wrote Lewis Carroll in *Alice in Wonderland*. As drawn by John Tenniel, a face you could never forget.

FOREWORD

No. 4: Puss in Boots The timeless hero of the classic fairy tale in its countless versions.

No. 5: Felix The star of the first "talkie" cartoon.

No. 6: Krazy Kat George Herriman's masterpiece of a comic strip.

No. 7: Mehitabel Archy's sidekick ("I was once Cleopatra"), created by Don Marquis.

No. 8: Edgar Allan Poe's *The Black Cat*

No. 9: Webster. P. G. Wodehouse's alcoholic cat

No. 10: Hamlet Legendary resident of the Algonquin Hotel lobby in New York.

—J.C. Suarès

As I was going to St. Ives,

I met a man with seven wives.

Each wife had seven sacks,

each sack had seven cats,

each cat had seven kits:

kits, cats, sacks and wives,

how many were going to St. Ives?

ANONYMOUS

CLAUDIA GORMAN
A Mother's Love
Pleasant Valley, New York, 1994

DAVID McENERY
CAT IN SHADES, 1993

This is the male kitten of a friend's cat's litter.
He was the most outgoing of all of them, a real showcat.

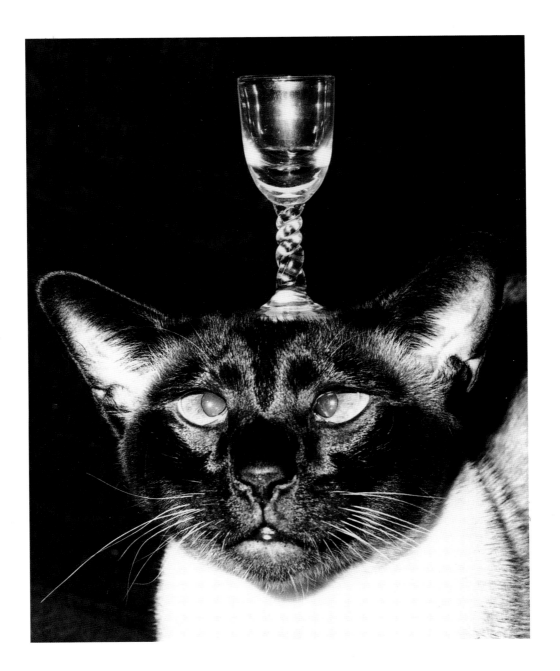

The Cat only grinned when it saw Alice. It looked good-natured, she thought:
still it had very long claws and a good many teeth, so she felt that it ought to be
treated with respect. "Cheshire Puss," she began, rather timidly, as she did not at all
know whether it would like the name: however, it only grinned a little wider.
"Come, it's pleased so far," thought Alice, and she went on. "Would you tell me,
please, which way I ought to go from here?"
"That depends a good deal on where you want to go," said the Cat.
"I don't much care where——" said Alice.
"Then it doesn't matter which way you go," said the Cat.
"——so long as I get somewhere," Alice added as an explanation.
"Oh, you're sure to do that," said the Cat, "if only you walk long enough."
Alice felt that this could not be denied, so she tried another question.
"What sort of people live around here?"
"In that direction," the Cat said, waving its right paw round, "lives a Hatter and in
that direction," waving the other paw, "lives a March Hare. Visit either you like:
they're both mad."
"But I don't want to go among mad people," Alice remarked.
"Oh, you can't help that," said the Cat. "We're all mad here. I'm mad. You're mad."
"How do you know I'm mad?" said Alice.
"You must be," said the Cat, "or you wouldn't be here."

LEWIS CARROLL
Alice's Adventures in Wonderland

WALTER CHANDOHA
CHESHIRE CAT, 1972

*I'm fascinated by the idea of a grinning cat. This was Smiley, one of our cats,
and his expression is as close to the Cheshire cat as I've come.*

MARILAIDE GHIGLIANO
OUTSKIRTS OF ROME, ITALY, 1991

"I got rained out photographing the ruins
at Ostia Antica and stepped into a pizzeria
and ordered a pie. When it arrived, a stray
cat showed up to beg for some pizza. Later,
when he had eaten more than I and was
taking it easy, I snapped his picture."

A Cat, hearing that there were some sick Birds in the neighborhood, got himself up as a doctor and set off to pay a house call. When he arrived at their home he called out to ask how the occupants were getting on. "Very well, thank you," came the reply, "if only you would go away."

AESOP
The Cat and the Birds

JAN RIETZ
CAT ON BIRDHOUSE, 1987

This was taken when my cat Millie was already ten years old. Even though Millie is a feminine name, he was a very male cat. He was a nice cat too, and an optimist—he was sure that the birds would fly right into his mouth as they headed for the birdhouse.

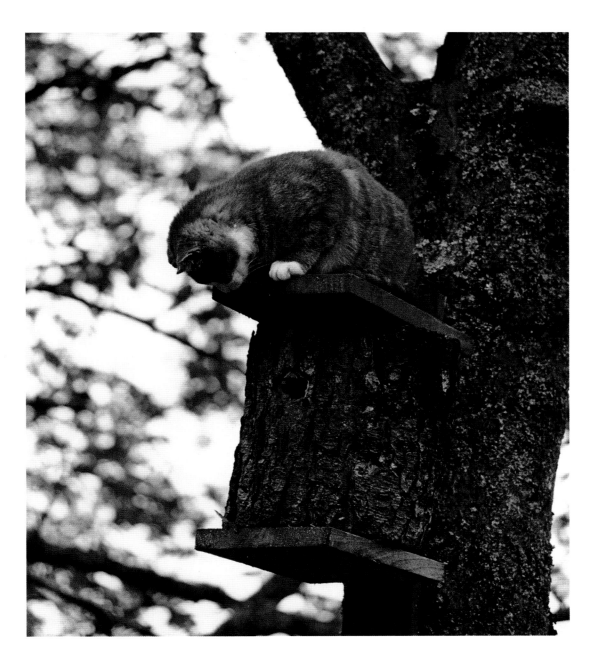

do you think that i would change

my present freedom to range

for a castle or moated grange

wotthehell wotthehell

cage me and i d go frantic

my life is so romantic

capricious and corybantic

and i m toujours gai toujours gai

DON MARQUIS
the song of mehitabel

GUY LE QUERREC
VILLE JUIF, 1975

Taken in a suburb near Paris.

22

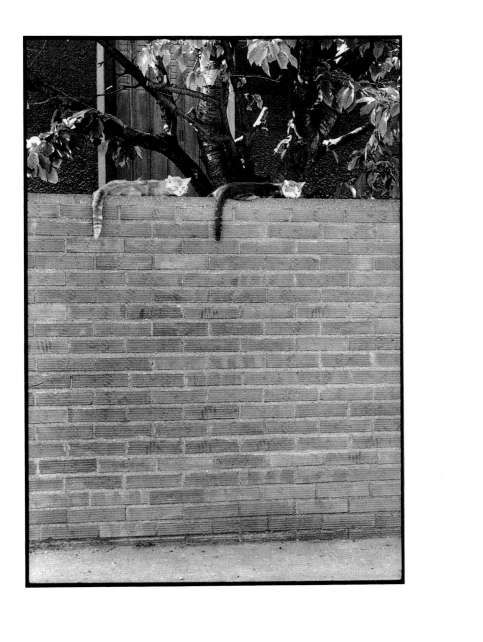

A kitten is so flexible that she is almost double; the hind parts are equivalent to another kitten with which the forepart plays. She does not discover that her tail belongs to her until you tread on it.

HENRY DAVID THOREAU

WALTER CHANDOHA
Washing Up
Long Island, New York, 1960

WALTER CHANDOHA
Persian in a Glass
Long Island, New York, 1961

PHOTOGRAPHER UNKNOWN
Root Beer Tabby
U.S., c. 1955

overleaf:
WALTER CHANDOHA
At the Sink
Huntington, Long Island, 1962

Balmain, my Burmese cat, thinks she's the head of the style police. She won't go near a person in a bad outfit, even if they're my honored guest. She sits in the alcove outside the living room, staring at them and making them feel incredibly insecure. My partner Chris used to wear Harris tweed jackets, and we all told him they looked ludicrous. But he wouldn't listen. So Balmain took the matter into her own hands. When Chris left his jacket on a chair one afternoon, Balmain methodically shredded it to rags. Issue resolved.

STEVEN MOY, SHOE DESIGNER, LONDON

RIGHT:
DAVID McENERY
MAXWELL HIDING,
BEAULIEU, FRANCE, 1996
"Maxwell, a very dignified English cat, does not like visitors.
Whenever there's a gathering, he hides in the old cottage
on our grounds and just peeks out at us from the screen
door as if to say, 'Go home, all of you.'"

OVERLEAF:
DONNA RUSKIN
BLACK AND WHITE KITTEN,
LAKE COMO, ITALY, 1994
"This kitten, whom I found crouched atop a wall in a town
north of Lake Como, was very skittish. I'm amazed he
stayed around as long as he did."

Holiday Advice

Two things that should never be left alone together:

a kitten and a just-ornamented Christmas tree.

DAVE ATKINS

SCREENWRITER

MANHATTAN

WALTER CHANDOHA
Now What
Huntington, Long Island, 1962

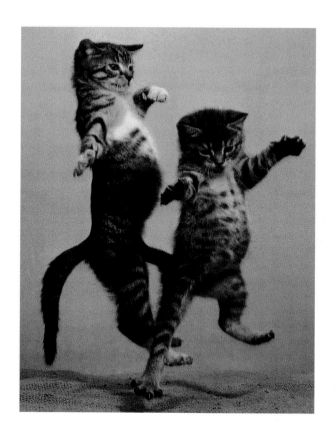

YLLA
Kittens in the Air
New York City, 1951

right:
PHOTOGRAPHER UNKNOWN
Hang On
Philadelphia, c. 1942

WALTER CARLOCK
Untitled
Ramsey, New Jersey, 1940

Opposite:
WALTER CHANDOHA
Paula Chandoha and Our Kitten Smiling
Long Island, New York, 1956
"The kitten was called Smiling for obvious reasons.
He was about eight weeks old here, the little mayor
of our city of daughters and cats."

Kook, my Siamese kitten, has prevented me from getting any sleep for the last three weeks. He has discovered that he has claws. At around midnight, just when I am trying to finally fall asleep, he gets wild. He likes to free-climb the curtains all the way up to the rods and then try to kill the curtain rings. I hear them rattling under his busy paws, and then I know I'm in for it. The next thing that happens is that he comes flying through the air, having propelled himself off a curtain rod, and lands on my bed—usually right on top of me, with all four paws extended. He also likes to leap onto my shirt and then rappel down my pant leg. Serves me right, I suppose, for those long hours I leave him alone when I go teach my slow fellow-humans how to climb.

CARL STERLING, CLIMBING INSTRUCTOR, BOSTON

RIGHT:
DAVID McENERY
HER SURROGATE, BEAULIEU, FRANCE, 1996
"Claude, our neighbor, had adopted a small Siamese
kitten whose mother had been hit by a car. I was visiting
Claude one afternoon when I noticed the kitten had taken
a fancy to the cat statue in the window. 'Perhaps,' said
Claude, 'it replaces her mother.'"

OVERLEAF:
KARL BADEN
RADAR CAT, RHODE ISLAND, 1993
"At a cat show, one of the problems is finding a way to
integrate foreground and background. But this cat
obviously didn't care a whit about the background."

WALTER CHANDOHA
Let Us In
Huntington, Long Island, 1962

NICK NICHOLS
WASHINGTON STATE, 1985

Taken in the cat-food testing quarters of the Carnation Company.

OVERLEAF: SCHOOL OF PHOTOGRAPHY,
NEWCASTLE UPON TYNE
MAKE YOUR MOVE, c. 1957

A gag shot set up with two burly players: Muskie, on the white side, and fellow Domestic Shorthair Tiggie, his opponent.

For having done duty and received blessing he begins to consider himself.

For this he performs in ten degrees.

For first he looks upon his fore-paws to see if they are clean.

For secondly he kicks up behind to clear away there.

For thirdly he works it upon stretch with the fore-paws extended.

For fourthly he sharpens his paws by wood.

For fifthly he washes himself.

For sixthly he rolls upon wash.

For seventhly he fleas himself, that he may not be interrupted upon the beat.

For eighthly he rubs himself against a post.

For ninthly he looks up for his instructions.

For tenthly he goes in quest for food.

CHRISTOPHER SMART
Jubilate Agno

WALTER CHANDOHA
OH, THAT FEELS GOOD, 1955

When we lived on Long Island I got my first cat, Loco—a very resourceful fellow.
He liked to sharpen his claws on the bark, as cats do. Then, always wanting to get more
for his money, he'd turn around to scratch his back.

THOMAS WESTER
Consolation at the Cat Show
Nybro, Sweden, 1984

The trouble with a

kitten is that

eventually it becomes a cat

OGDEN NASH

LAURA STRAUS
Pippi
City Island, New York, 1999

overleaf:
THOMAS WESTER
Distraction
Vagnhärad, Sweden, 1992

ANDREA MOHIN
Spike and His Pal
Washington, D.C., 1991
"We had just moved to this house and this was
Spike's first introduction to the backyard. You could say that
the cement cat solidified his introduction to the outdoors."

MICHAEL NICHOLS

UNTITLED, BERKELEY, CALIFORNIA, 1980s

"Pearl was a male cat that we captured as a feral kitten and tried to make into a housecat. In the five years we had him, he never really became domesticated, but just roamed wild into our loft. For the past two years I've been photographing tigers, and I really don't see much difference between tigers and cats."

DAVID McENERY

BOSS CAT, LOS ANGELES, CALIFORNIA, 1994

"Our son's cat, Jack, weighs sixteen pounds and eats everything in sight. This is the way he likes to sit on the couch. He is a true couch potato."

Sympathy Cat

WALTER CHANDOHA
Chiara and Ginger
Annandale, New Jersey, 1966

The year after my mother died, I would stay home alone on the weekends just trying to deal with it. I had this one cat named Nori-San who was black with a white triangle on his chest. He had green eyes and a sweet little voice. Normally he was pretty friendly—nothing remarkable. But during this time he became extremely loving. He'd come and nuzzle me or lick my ear, or he'd try to distract me with his antics. He'd keep at it until I cheered up. Once I got over my blue period, he reverted back to his old self, stealing my jewelry and hiding it under the sofa. One morning at 4 a.m. I realized I'd lost my watch and when Nori-San ran by, he had the watch in his mouth. I followed him into the living room and under the couch he had this little stash. There was everything I thought I'd lost. And he was perfectly willing to give it back. He was a very special cat.

MISSY ROGERS, CLOTHING DESIGNER

DAVID MCENERY
LOST NOTE, 1992

That's Lovejoy, our own kitten. He's a very curious cat.
You just leave him alone and let him go.

Domesticity

I rescued two kittens living in the barn on my mother's farm and brought them back to New York. My place was a loft, one big room. For exercise they'd have daily indoor steeplechases. Their course was always the same. They'd start on my bed, race across the floor and over my desk, knocking anything they could to the floor, then leap six feet onto the dish rack, with extra points if something fell and made a huge clatter, then into the sink to splash dishwater everywhere. Then they'd leap back to the floor, circle the columns at full tilt and make a mad dash back to the finish line, which was at the top of the silk curtains. The girl kitten, a real toughie, always won.

CAROLANNE PATTERSON

ARTIST

MANHATTAN

PHOTOGRAPHER UNKNOWN
Who's the Fairest One of All?
U.S., c. 1945

WALTER CHANDOHA
GREENWICH VILLAGE, NEW YORK, 1954

My friend Mabel Schezleri was the cat columnist for the old World Telegram.
Her nom de plume was Henrietta Hitchcock. One day we were just fooling around and her cat
got onto the kitchen table and sat in the bowl.

OVERLEAF: WALTER CHANDOHA
HERE'S LOOKING AT YOU, NEW YORK, 1956

This was taken in a New York apartment. The kitten, a Siamese,
just rushed up to the mirror and started staring.

Kitty Gimmicks

Kittens are like old comedians. They always use the same shticks. There's the scaredy-kitten stance, the vampy butt-in-the-air move, the you're-so-boring-I-could-die glare, the monster-under-the-sheets attack, and of course the I'm-so-little-how-could-you-possibly-get-mad look. The gimmicks work, so why change them?

VARDA MILLER

ASPIRING COMIC

CHICAGO

JAYNE HINDS BIDAUT
"Kitten," from the "Animalerie" Series
Paris, 1987

Maurice

WALTER CHANDOHA
Minguina and Kitten
Huntington, Long Island, 1952

Maurice's mother climbed into my lap to have him and three other kittens. Maurice slept with me every night from that day until he was well into his second year. One day, I had to go to Puerto Rico for a long weekend to work on a film. When I got back, he seemed totally disheveled and bleary-eyed. Unused to sleeping by himself, he had paced around the whole time.

As he got older he grew quite large, to about twenty pounds. And he was clumsy. Whenever he'd see me, he'd flip over on his back and the whole room would shake.

Needless to say, he slept with me for the rest of his life.

J.C. SUARÈS

No matter how much cats fight, there

always seem to be plenty of kittens.

ABRAHAM LINCOLN

preceding pages:
PHOTOGRAPHER UNKNOWN
Dashboard Kitty
Denver, Colorado, 1946

right:
THOMAS WESTER
My Fantastic Chance
Vagnhärad, Sweden, 1992

PHOTOGRAPHER UNKNOWN
PARIS, FRANCE, 1963

At the annual show presented by the Cat Circle of
Paris, this Blue Persian makes his first appearance.
The cat's young mistress, however, thinks more of him
as a playmate than as a prospective champion.

(Original caption, circa 1963)

PHOTOGRAPHER UNKNOWN
LONDON, ENGLAND, DATE UNKNOWN

Little Gordon Peters, two years old, carrying his Blue
Persian kitten, Minnow, into the Royal Horticultural Hall.

PHOTOGRAPHER UNKNOWN
Desiree Sampson and Her Cat Billy
London, 1950

LEFT:

JOHN DRYSDALE
PEEK-A-BOO,
LONDON, ENGLAND, 1990

"The pianist for a London toddlers'
dancing class used to bring her
cat, which always distracted the
kids. The cat, on the other
hand, never seemed too interested.
One afternoon, while it was grooming itself — typically oblivious to
the goings-on — one little girl
decided an inverted view of the cat
was far more interesting than an
arabesque. True to form, the cat
ignored the entire spectacle."

How to Bond with a Dog

One of my own cats, a champagne tabby named Stain, fell in love with my dog over the course of a month when they were both in the house a lot. It was the rainy season in Arizona, and the animals preferred the confines of the house to the stormy outside. Stain had never given the dog much attention. But suddenly, he seemed overcome by an incredible desire to spend every minute, waking or not, at her side. She is a gentle, playful German Shepherd, more curious than aggressive. At first she'd lie on the floor, her side against the front door in her customary way, and Stain would come marching up, his tail held kitten-high, and head right for her face. He'd brush himself against her two or three times until finally she gave him a lick. Thus encouraged, he'd come back for more, beginning to purr and playfully box her nose with a paw, until finally she began to wag her tail. When he sensed she'd accepted him, he steadied himself and jumped clear onto her back, wedging himself between dog and door. If she got up to find privacy, he'd rush between her legs, slowing her down, lying on his back and poking up at her. After a week, she relented. From then on she expected him to be at her side, and he was. At mealtimes, on walks, even when I took her for a jog—Stain would follow close behind, never letting her out of his adoring sight.

Jane Martin

Thomas Wester
Natural Enemies
Stockholm, Sweden, 1984

Overleaf:
Thomas Wester
Natural Enemies Continued
Stockholm, Sweden, 1984

Batty, my cat, is enormous, but she moves pretty fast. The only thing is that she sometimes gets stuck in places. My friend came over with her dog, and Batty hates dogs. First she puffed herself up to twice her size, which made her look absolutely obese. But she thought she looked really tough. Then, when the dog didn't get scared, she charged. The dog didn't move. So at the last minute Batty veered away and dashed behind the armchair. Somehow she got herself wedged in there, though I didn't know it. I just thought she was hiding. Hours later, my friend and the dog had gone, and I heard a plaintive little meow coming from behind the chair. There was Batty, stuck in the funniest position, all four paws off the ground and her belly stuck between the back of the chair and the wall. She had kept her cool until the dog was gone rather than admit she needed help.

DEANNA CHUI, LAWYER, BROOKLYN

RIGHT:
ANONYMOUS
WHITE CAT, U.S., 1950s
At home on the moving edge of a rolling wooden ball, this white cat keeps its cool.

THOMAS WESTER
Kitten Climbing Blue Jeans
Utlängan, Blekinge Archipelago, Sweden, 1983

right:
Kitten on Telephone Pole
Skärblaka, Sweden, 1984

DAVID McENERY
Daisy at the Sweater
Los Angeles, California, 1994

overleaf:
TERRY DeROY GRUBER
Chapin Nursery School
Upper East Side, New York City, 1979

ROBIN SCHWARTZ
BROOKLYN, NY, 1996

"Fat cat Walter loves to watch the water swirl in the toilet bowl.

ROBIN SCHWARTZ
BROOKLYN, NY, 1996

Walter gets a big hug from his owner, Angela.

JOHN DRYSDALE
HASLEMERE, ENGLAND, 1979

Marvin began life as a sickly kitten who was fed from an eyedropper.
He grew up on a gourmet diet of venison, salmon from Scotland, steak,
chicken, and vitamins with ice cream. Marvin refused all cat food and
preferred a ride in the family's vintage chauffeur-driven car to chasing
mice in the garden. Marvin always traveled on his own velvet cushion.

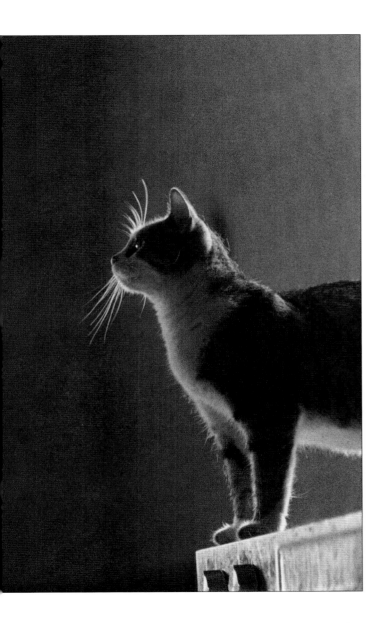

THOMAS WESTER
Maj Stina Larsson
Yttemas Roslagen,
Sweden, 1984

My cat Aretha hates loud rock, but she loves the sound of a good song. If I go to the piano and play something she likes, she'll come over to listen. She prefers something low-key, but she'll really get into the blues if she's in the right mood. She doesn't mind guitar, though she prefers it acoustic. And she hates the drums. I had a piano student who liked her a lot, and he used to bring her treats, like a can of tuna or sardines. After Aretha devoured the entire thing, she'd get up on top of the piano and roll over onto her side to listen to him play. She'd loll on top of that piano and purr for an hour while my student practiced his rolling bass lines.

S.A. SLIM, MUSICIAN, NEW ORLEANS

RIGHT:
DAVID McENERY
HIGH C,
LOS ANGELES, CALIFORNIA, 1994
"This is our cat, Lovejoy. He'd fallen asleep inside the guitar case, and when he woke up, he gave a big yawn. Anything we leave laying around, Lovejoy adopts and falls asleep in it."

KARL BADEN

LOVER, BOSTON, 1992

"This cat was rolling around, trying to seduce me.
Fortunately, or maybe unfortunately, I resisted."

RIGHT:

ANN FINNELL

SAM, NEW YORK CITY, 1997

"Sam, our domestic shorthair tabby, knows when I'm
taking his picture. He likes to get into as feline a position as possible, preferably on my favorite armchair,
and do a little on-camera demonstration of how impos-
sibly supple and adorable cats are — as opposed to
people, who can't quite stretch out the same way."

ABOVE:

ROBIN SCHWARTZ
CHINA,
RUTHERFORD, NEW JERSEY, 1996

"China, a domestic shorthair, was very
shy the whole time I was around.
Here she's about two years old."

Romance

ROBIN SCHWARTZ
Noah and Nathaniel
Hoboken, New Jersey, 1994

I know cats feel differently. But they have their own kind of romance. When they fall in love, it's deeply. The Big Daddy around my house is Sir Oliver, a handsome and distinguished tabby who loves attention. One of my females, Glistening Sylvia, is an absolute flirt at nine years old, and she will not leave Oliver alone. She hugs him, kisses him, tries to snuggle underneath him when he naps, and follows him everywhere. When he requests a little privacy by putting out a paw, she sits a few feet away and stares at him adoringly. When they lie together on the throw rug in the hall, she'll growl to keep everyone else away. She wants him for himself, and I think he loves it. I've never seen him admonish her.

MARGE BEEBE, ANIMAL BEHAVIORIST
AND BREEDER OF MAINE COON CATS

I had rather be a kitten, and cry mew

Than one of these same meter ballad mongers

WILLIAM SHAKESPEARE

YLLA
Tico-Tico Encounters a Cat
New York City, c. 1950

KRITINA LEE KNIEF
SINBAD AND ALFIE, 1985

These are my cats in Weehawken, New Jersey,
where I lived then. I had just recently taken in Alfie,
the orphan kitten. Sinbad, who was usually not
very cordial to other cats, just fell in love with Alfie.
He'd let her do anything to him.

OVERLEAF: TERRY deROY GRUBER
WHOOPSIE AND POOPSIE,
NEW YORK, 1979

These are the cats of the Offset Printing Company,
on Broome Street in Soho. They have a lot of
Russian Blue blood. I'd heard a lot about them, but
every time I went to take their picture they were out.
The sixth time I showed up, they were both in. As soon
as I made the shot they took off again. Some of the
customers call them the Bureaucats, since they do
nothing around there but hold up the operation.

PHOTOGRAPHER UNKNOWN
The Great Cat Round-up
Bowling Green, New York, March 28, 1925
Jack Jagerke is the proud captor of three of the thousand-
odd stray cats that were rounded up by the Bowling Green
Neighborhood Association and then adopted as pets.

PHOTOGRAPHER UNKNOWN
How Infantile Paralysis is Spread
1916
A child plays with a stray who was caught while feeding
on garbage. Such contact, it was believed in 1916,
could endanger a child's life.

DONNA RUSKIN
GREENVILLE ARMS TABBY,
CATSKILLS, NEW YORK, 1991

"This shorthaired tabby, resident cat at a bed-and-breakfast in
the Catskill Mountains, thinks nothing of lying straight across the
path of oncoming guests. His excuse may be the sunshine, but does
he get a kick out of watching guests step gingerly around him?"

MIKAEL BERTMAR
CAT AND SHADOW,
GOTHENBORG, SWEDEN, 1990

"One very sunny summer day, I was walking through a
nice Gothenborg neighborhood. It's an area with both smaller
villas and bigger houses, where everything is very tidy. I saw
this cat stalking around, accompanied by his wilder shadow,
and I thought, here's somebody's ordinary housecat feeling just
like a tiger. After I took the picture the cat came up and
rubbed against my leg, and seemed domestic once again. I like to
think he was thanking me for sharing his secret life."

ROBIN SCHWARTZ
BROOKLYN, NY, MID-1980S

"Whitey [right] had been my
cat since I was ten years old.
He was my cat brother. I used to
sleep with him in my arms. On
trips Tobey [my other cat] rode in a
carrier, but it would have been an
insult to put Whitey in a cage."

Cat was a real oddity. The others didn't know what to make of him at all. He lived in a hollow tree in the wood. Every night, when the rest of the creatures were sound asleep, he retired to the depths of his tree—then such sounds, such screechings, yowlings, wailings! The bats that slept upside-down all day long in the hollows of the tree branches awoke with a start and fled with their wing-tips stuffed into their ears. It seemed to them that Cat was having the worst nightmares ever—ten at a time! But no. Cat was tuning his violin.

....

TED HUGHES
How the Cat Became

ROBIN SCHWARTZ
SAFRAM SPHYNX KITTENS, YORKTOWN HEIGHTS,
NEW YORK, 1993

I went to Safram, Sandra Adler's cattery, to see her new litter. They were very young, and very unkitten-like. Rumpelstiltskin is the one sitting up. The Sphynx is a rare breed: there are less than six hundred in the world, though they've been around for a hundred years. According to the breed's historians, they're descended from a feral cat on the streets of Toronto, or from a Minnesota barn cat. They used to just appear as a mutant gene in litters, but now they're bred very carefully. As kittens, they feel like warm suede. Sandra says that the word 'alien' seems more appropriate than cat.

Cats are always elegant.

NED ROSEN, NY, 1997
Dinah, named after the cat in *Alice in Wonderland*, is
three years old and weighs about seventeen pounds.

The Girl Next Door

DONNA RUSKIN
Untitled
New York, 1989

One of my cats had an affair with the female kitten next door. It was a presexual, childhood affair. They would romp and cuddle. But as soon as she got fixed, he stopped getting along with her. She seemed devastated for about a day. She came to my door and wailed. Then the next day she had a new beau.

ANNE MARLOWE, WRITER

KRITINA LEE KNIEF
CAT POSING, NEW YORK, 1992

This is Alfie, who arrived on my doorstep nine years ago. I'd just lost a cat and my friends found her. They asked me if I could just watch her overnight. Of course that stretched out to a little longer. I can always count on her to stay in one place.

PHOTOGRAPHER UNKNOWN
CAT'S-EYE VIEW, C. 1945

So many gag photos were sent over the wire to newspapers across the country that a cat's most unnatural behavior became perfectly unsurprising. Still, no one will ever know what really sent this large American Shorthair to the viewfinder of the Speed Graphic, or whether—a moment later—the tripod stayed up.

"What I've got against cats," said a Lemon Sour, speaking feelingly,

as one brooding on a private grievance, "is their unreliability.

They lack candor and are not square shooters. You get your cat and you

call him Thomas or George, as the case may be. So far, so good.

Then one morning you wake up and find six kittens in the hat box and

you have to re-open the whole matter...."

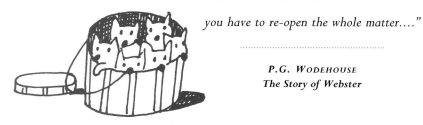

P.G. WODEHOUSE
The Story of Webster

PHOTOGRAPHER UNKNOWN
MAURICE CHEVALIER AND CAT, C. 1925

*The young French crooner and his slightly cross-eyed partner sport twin straw boaters
for this portrait of two dandies.*

ABOVE:

**UNIDENTIFIED
CLEVER CAT,
NEW YORK, 1940s**

This clever tuxedo-patterned cat, according
to his trainer A. Coxe, can juggle with
figures up to six, and can add, multiply,
and subtract. He gives his answers by
sitting down on the right square.

RIGHT:

**UNIDENTIFIED
GOING THROUGH HOOPS,
NEW YORK, 1940s**

Trainer A. Coxe and his assistant
hold the hoops while a spotted
shorthair leaps neatly through them.

THOMAS WESTER
A Warm Place
Stockholm, Sweden, 1990

overleaf:
DAVID McENERY
Satisfaction
Brighton, England, 1992

ROBIN SCHWARTZ
Potatoes and Stigby
Hoboken, New Jersey, 1995

ROBIN SCHWARTZ
Jonah and Noah
Hoboken, New Jersey, 1993

The Love of a Pride

THOMAS WESTER
Fence Romance
Dalhem Gotland, Sweden, 1984

My Maine Coons always surprise me. They're pride cats, descended from wildcats in Maine. Most domestic cats are descended from North African wildcats, which were lone hunters. Maine's wildcats live in prides, and not only accept each other's company, they want it. To make a stronger distinction think of dogs, who are pack animals. A pack animal will find a morsel of food and steal away so he can eat it all by himself. A pride animal will bring it back for everyone else. My cats not only bring home the bacon, they make a big show of it and invite each other to share in the wealth. Then they lie in happy heaps and just purr.

I had a kitten who once got into a big mess and I had to wash him off. So I took him over to the sink and started rinsing his fur. I was very gentle but a kitten is a kitten and he started to scream. All the other cats heard him. Before I knew it I was surrounded by the pride. They were so concerned that they tried to stop me by putting their arms around my legs. If you've ever felt a cat put their arms around your leg, you know the message. It's "Stop, right now. I insist." I had a choice: risk scratches and worse, or stop. I got the kitten rinsed off enough to be safe, and put him down. Immediately, the pride ushered him into the next room and began to clean him themselves.

MARGE BEEBE, ANIMAL BEHAVIORIST AND BREEDER OF MAINE COON CATS

Silence of a Siamese

KRITINA LEE KNIEF
Jasmine and Sabu
Chicago, 1991

My neighbor has a Siamese, Ethel Merman, who is very vocal. I can hear them talking to each other. He's been sick, and recently had to leave for a week to have some tests, and I fed Ethel Merman. Everyday I'd let myself in and walk into my neighbor's kitchen and Ethel would come running in, chattering away. Then she'd stop and give me this look. Just a long, steady look. And she'd be silent until I left. When he came back, the reunion was very emotional. I know. I heard it.

RITSUKO UCHIDA, ARTIST

KRITINA LEE KNIEF
CAT IN LEATHER JACKET, NEW YORK, 1992

*His name is Buddy Rodriguez. He's a friend's kitten, bought from someone
at a flea market holding a "kittens for sale" sign. He was perfect—really into cuddling.
He would fall asleep all the time. We had to keep him awake.*

OVERLEAF: LARS PETER ROOS
BURMA KATTER, STOCKHOLM, 1988

*My friend Peter put his Burmese cats, Lotus and Julia, on the double doors because he knew they
liked to sit there. They were sisters from the same litter, and the real owners of Peter's apartment.*

Getting Underfoot

I breed Persians, who are very self-possessed. The kittens are so cute you could scream, but they hate to be fawned over. One of my favorites, Money, now a champion, was a gray furball as a kitten, always getting into things. He crept into my husband Mike's sock drawer one morning. Mike's very groggy when he wakes up. He tried to unroll Money and put him on his feet, which resulted in quite a scene.

MERYL SHAWNESSEY

CAT BREEDER

PENNSYLVANIA

KRITINA LEE KNIEF
Persian Kitten Squooshing Hat
Boston, Massachusetts, 1991

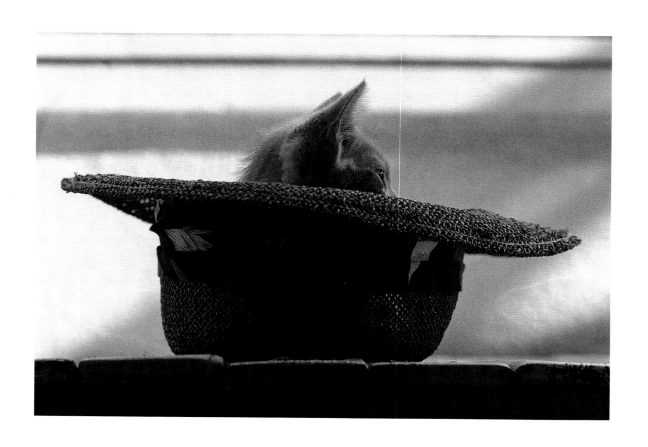

DAVID MCENERY
HAT CAT, 1992

There's a pet store in Santa Monica that lends me kittens for a few days.
This was one of the loaners.

KRITINA LEE KNIEF
KITTEN IN HAT BOX, 1991

This was taken in Boston for my children's book, Alphabet Cats. *The little guy's name is
Muddy Waters. His breeder, who's known for her Persians, names all her cats after musicians.
We put fifteen kittens and cats in this set, and they had a great romp, scattering the boxes and
crushing the hats. It may have been work to us, but it was a playground to them.*

The Cat Who Came to Work

Thomas Wester
Untitled
Stockholm, Sweden, 1984

Of all the cats I've ever known, Polar Star is the most lovable. He's named after Polar Bear, the cat who came for Christmas, who was also a wonderful cat but in a different way. Polar Star is also white, a big guy with six toes on each paw. Someone on Martha's Vineyard just threw him out of her house at the end of the summer. And now I want her to know what she's missing, because he's the most all-around lovable cat I have seen in my life. When I first met him, he came and put his paw on me, and I was blown away. I always tease people that they taught him to do that. The Board members love him. The whole office loves him. Anyone who comes in, Polar Star has to sit in their lap and find out what they're up to. Since he's been here, more than 300 people have asked me if they could adopt him. But I'd never give him up. He's affectionate, philosophical and sweet: everything you could ever want in one cat.

Cleveland Amory, president and founder, The Fund for Animals

174

TERRY deROY GRUBER
Humbert Humbert, from the *Fat Cats* Series
California, 1980
"Humbert Humbert belonged to
the Argyle Academy—an all-girls school."

Tender Ziggy

THOMAS WESTER
Curious Man and Cat
Stockholm, Sweden, 1988

My sister has this old cat named Ziggy, a big fat alley cat. He's usually very disdainful and haughty when there are a lot of people in a room. He either glares at you or makes himself scarce. Well, one day I was visiting and was only one of many people in the room, so of course the cat was being very snooty and I was being snooty back. Then, suddenly, everyone else walked out. We were alone. I was on the sofa, he was prowling the floor. And I have to say that he made the first move. He climbed up to me and put his paws on my shoulders, just like an embrace, and then he just stared me in the face. I felt an intense love coming from him then. We touched noses in a delicate, intimate gesture. Then someone came into the room and it was over. I guess he only loves people one on one, in private. Then he's actually very tender.

SPENCER BECK, WRITER

ALFRED GESCHEIDT
Ciba
New York, 1958
"I had two Siamese then: Columbo and Ciba, named
after a company I did a lot of work for. We'd play on the roof,
which like most of the old tenement roofs, had a lot of nooks and
crannies. I was throwing a ball when it suddenly disappeared,
and Ciba with it. My heart sank. When I got around the corner
there she was, trying to get the ball out of the drainpipe."

Opposite:
PHOTOGRAPHER UNKNOWN
Animal Rescue League
1940

ABOVE AND RIGHT:
ROBIN SCHWARTZ
NEW YORK, NY, 1996

"This cat lives at Culver Pictures, a photo archive.
He looks as if he is smiling but actually, he's hissing;
he didn't care for the flash on my camera."

Said the Parrot to the Pussycat

I adopted a gray tabby, one of those remote, attractive types that won't tell you how they're feeling. I named him Redford. And I brought him into a house that already had a dog, Oprah, and a parrot named Cassandra. I was a little nervous about creating my own food chain, so I tried to keep them separated. Redford and Oprah kept their distance, but Redford would not stay away from Cassandra. Her cage was in the living room and that's where he wanted to be. He was fascinated by her. I was really nervous I'd come home from work to a mess of feathers.

One day I was in the living room when Redford came in. Cassandra had her eye on him too. She cocked her head in that "I see you" way. I held my breath. And what did Redford do? He jumped onto the edge of the sofa and hooked a claw into Cassandra's cage to hold it fast. If the cage door opened, death in a minute. But Cassandra? She made this noise. Not an alarm but a low chirp. Kind of seductive. She sidestepped down her perch toward the cat. Stupid bird! Then they touched noses. Or beak and nose. I couldn't believe this! They did it again and again.

"Cassandra," I called out. "Are you all right?" Usually I'd get an answer. But Cassandra was busy. Redford was purring and turning his head upside down to get a different look at her and she was delighted. She poked lightly at him with her beak and fluttered her wings prettily and bobbed up and down. Then I understood. Maybe poor Redford had a parrot in his previous life. Maybe Cassandra didn't know any better. But there was no food chain involved.

Their attachment deepened. She'd leave her cage to be at his side. They ate together, talked together, slept—spent almost all their time together. Cassandra would settle next to Redford and he'd put his arm around her. They were so gentle you'd swear they were under a spell. I wish I had a picture.

TESSA SMITH, ACTRESS

ROBIN SCHWARTZ
Ricky and Tequilla
Teaneck, New Jersey, 1995

Preceding pages:
DOREEN AND THOMAS VYSE
Cairns, Queensland,
Australia, circa 1986
"Himmy, 46 pounds 15.25 ounces, was like a person, not like a cat; you could talk to him. Regarding weight, he never ate more than eight to ten ounces of food a day. All of a sudden, he just started to grow."

"O my Enemy and Wife of my Enemy and Mother of my Enemy,"

said the Cat, "it is I: for you have spoken three words in my praise,

and now I can drink the warm white milk three times a day for always

and always and always. But still I am the Cat who walks by himself,

and all places are alike to me." Then the Woman laughed

and set the Cat a bowl of warm white milk and said, "O Cat, you are

as clever as a man, but remember that your bargain was not made

with the Man or the Dog, and I do not know what they will do when

they come home." "What is that to me?" said the Cat. "If I have

my place in the Cave by the fire and my warm white milk three times

a day. I do not care what the Man or the Dog can do."

RUDYARD KIPLING
The Cat Who Walked by Himself

PHOTOGRAPHER UNKNOWN
MILKTIME, C. 1940

A farmer's tabby gets his customary treat during a milking—one of the countless cat photographs sent over the wire during the heyday of small-town Americana scenes.

My black and white cat, Roland, adopted me. He's so handsome—with enormous yellow eyes and a majestic ruff around his neck—that I just had to take him in. I was eating breakfast on my front porch when he came galloping out of nowhere, obviously very hungry. The problem was, at that point, that I had three adolescent dogs who were very disobedient, and a teenage son, and I was in the habit of raising my voice a bit. As in "Hey! Get your nose out of the refrigerator!" Or "Off the couch with those filthy feet!" Well, the dogs are used to it, and my son forgave me too, though he suggested I try a certain illegal herb to relax. But Roland immediately let me know that he, being a cat, would not tolerate such outbursts. One day I caught him sharpening his claws on a chair leg and yelled "Bad cat! Stop that now!" Instead Roland just turned his head and gave me a piercing stare. It was as if he were saying, "Excuse me? Just whom do you think you're talking to?"

LISE KLAMMER, NURSE, AMSTERDAM

RIGHT:
DAVID McENERY
STREET OF CATS, DINAN, FRANCE, 1994
"There is a street in Dinan that leads down to the port.
It's a very old street, twisting and cobblestoned. I
think everyone who lives on it must have a cat,
because they are everywhere you look. I noticed this
one peering at me as I took an afternoon walk."

Josephine

My cat saved my life. Not directly, but just by being her. When I was in the hospital, I was in a very sedated state for a while. I must have been told that I might not come out of it, because I was vaguely conscious that death was a prospect. I remember having end-of-life kind of dreams.

In my hazy state I sort of reviewed in my mind all the people I knew—my friends and relations. And I came to the conclusion that everybody would survive this. And then I got to my own family. I got to my kitten, Terry, and concluded that she was young enough to survive this. But then I got to Josephine, the older cat. What about Josephine? That question was ringing in my ears. I don't know what the timing of this was, but the doctor later told me that just about when he'd given up all hope, I turned around and started fighting for my life. And I figured out later that it was on the same day as I thought about Josephine that there was a change in all those dial readings.

I can't know for certain that the thought and the improvement were connected. But it seems to me that this was the only notion I had that said, "Charles, you have to pull out of this." As I say this, Josephine's sitting on my lap. She's sprawled out with one nail dug right into my skin through the ankle, and the other dug into the leather of my shoe. This is how she spends a lot of her time. Ever since I came back from the hospital, she's been more affectionate than she'd ever been before. She started this habit of following me everywhere. She will not let me out of her sight. If I have to go somewhere, she's invariably inside the door to the garage when I come back, and she gives me kind of a "whough"— almost like a bark. She absolutely thinks that I'm her person. I don't think anyone who's been near us has any doubt about that.

CHARLES SHEROVER, PHILOSOPHER

THOMAS WESTER
Norwegian Fisherman and His Cat
Vaeroy Lofoten, Norway, 1974

Previous pages:
PHOTOGRAPHER UNKNOWN
Place unknown, date unknown
"Letting the fat cat out of the bag!"

URSULA ANDRESS. 1962
Above: *The co-star of the first James Bond movie,* Dr. No, *with
Sean Connery, holds an Oriental Shorthair.*

JOAN COLLINS. 1957
Right: *A straw-hatted Joan Collins holds a kitten in her shirt
during the filming of* Island in the Sun.

They say that you can get a dog used to riding in a
car, but they don't say a thing about cats. I drive my
convertible hundreds of miles a month, going to visit my
boyfriend up in Charlotte, and no one has a better time
than my cat Josephina. I found her as a kitten in a rest
area along the highway, and thought oh, how awful, the
idea of a little helpless cat near all those giant racing cars.
But now I wonder if she was just looking for a ride. She
likes to stand on the passenger seat with her paws up on
the door, watching the world race by, and she hisses if a
car with a dog inside passes us. She likes to order French
fries from the drive-thru at McDonald's, and take-out grits
from Waffle House. I think she lives for being on the road,
because she never eats French fries or grits at home.

PORTIA CARRERA, STUDENT, ATLANTA

RIGHT:
UPI PHOTOGRAPHER
MITTEN THE EASY RIDER,
SAN PEDRO, CALIFORNIA, 1977
Owner Karl Mitchell takes his
young black cat Mitten, who loves
motorcycle riding, out for a spin.

Thomas Wester
Untitled
Stockholm, Sweden, 1984

THE SHADOW OF THE CAT. 1961
A black cat seeks revenge for her owner's murder.

THE BLACK CAT. 1934
Bela Lugosi co-starred with Boris Karloff for the first time in this loose adaptation of Edgar Allan Poe's story of a cat returning from the dead to haunt its master. The movie wound up having more to do with a story by director Edgar Ulmer than with Poe's tale, though a sleek black cat did appear. The title was changed to The Vanishing Body *when Universal released a second* Black Cat *in 1941.*

Sinbad

HAROLD M. LAMBERT
The Grooming Session
Philadelphia, c.1950

My cat Sinbad, who I got when he was a kitten along with his sister Salem, does this loving gesture I've never seen before: he sucks on my ear. I can hold him in my arms like a baby and he'll lean into my neck and suckle on my ear. It's a very intimate gesture. He can stay there for hours, completely content. Then he goes and finds Salem and they curl up together like a yin-yang symbol.

JENNIFER CHARLES, RECORDING ARTIST

DAVID McENERY
CATNAP II, 1992

*My wife, Pat, made the hammock. She's a great
hammock maker. The kitten thought so too.
They don't have hammocks at the pet store.*

OVERLEAF: WALTER CHANDOHA
TICKLING THE IVORIES, 1957

I guess the kitten liked the sound of the keys.

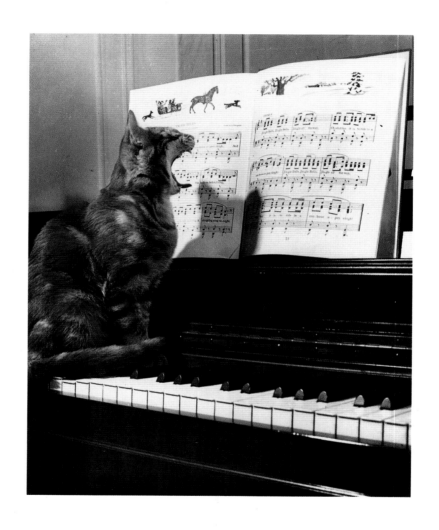

GEORGE W. GRAY
Singing Cat
New York, 1946
Rusty, the photographer's 6-month-old kitten,
rehearses a Christmas "Catenza."

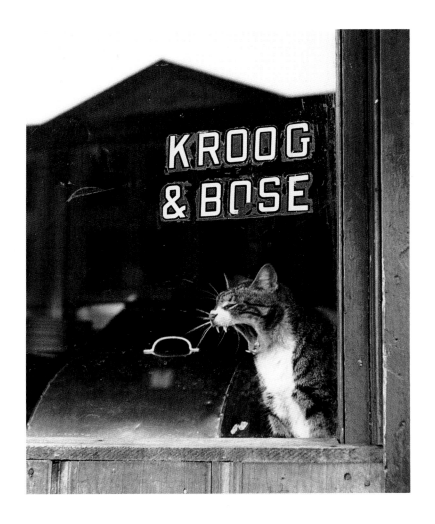

WALTER CHANDOHA
Guard Cat
New York, 1955
At the Fulton Fish Market, a store's cat keeps
a watchful eye on the street.

DAVID MCENERY
CATNAP I, 1979

That is a genuine English deck chair and those are my wife, Pat McEnery's, feet.
The picture was taken on our patio soon after I came to America. The kitten was borrowed.

RHUBARB. 1951
At fourteen pounds, Orangey the cat had enough presence to look imposing on a baseball diamond, but the camera angle helped. The leash was there in case the star decided to bolt.

The great charm of cats is their rampant

egotism, their devil-may-care attitude

toward responsibility, their disinclination

to earn an honest dollar...cats are disdainful of

everything but their own immediate interests...

ROBERTSON DAVIES
THE PAPERS OF SAMUEL MARCHBANKS

JUST G. MOLLER
JUTLAND, DENMARK, 1959
This fat cat drinks milk from a saucer or a baby
bottle. No matter, as long as lunch is forthcoming.

Cats are absolute individuals with

their own ideas about everything,

including the people they own.

JOHN DINGMAN
The Artistic Cat

JOYCE RAVID
NEW YORK, NY, 1976

"This is fat cat Brother and his 'keeper.'
Brother thinks it is impolite to ask his weight."

JESSIE TARBOX BEALS
Siamese Cat
c. 1905

Opposite:
YLLA
Face-off with Tabby
New York, c. 1950
A silent confrontation with a leader of what the
photographer called the "Feline Underworld."

THE BLACK CAT. 1941
Universal's second version of the Edgar Allen Poe story, a comedy-chiller, also featured Bela Lugosi. He played the caretaker for a woman who kept a crematorium for her beloved cats. Anne Gwynne played an innocent victim haunted at midnight by the feline villain.

It is a very inconvenient habit

of kittens (Alice had once made

the remark) that, whatever you

say to them, they always purr.

LEWIS CARROLL

JOAN BARON
Kitten at the Barre, Phyllis Goldman's Ballet Studio
Upper East Side, New York City, 1983

Mochi the Jungle Cat

PER WICHMANN
Kittens
Stockholm, Sweden, 1990

We come here maybe twice a year, more if we can get the time from touring, and our shack in the jungle is empty except for then. Mochi is a jungle cat, the same mixture of tortoiseshell and Siamese that a lot of cats in Puna, Hawaii, are—small and fierce, strong enough to kill a mongoose or a rat and live for days on nothing.

When we get here, she suddenly shows up. Every year. No one else ever sees her. And every year she shows up pregnant, as if she times her litters for our arrival, knowing somehow that when we're around, there's good food and good care. She moves right in in her quiet, sweet way, never pushing us, never demanding, just watching. Her belly swells bigger and bigger and of course we hand her all the extras from whatever meal we've made, and she never gets fussy or upset.

We are her guardians—her midwives—she seems to be saying, and she pays us back in affection. One by one on the first days we're all together here, she climbs into our laps and welcomes us. Then the routine is exactly as it has always been. The day we are all scheduled to leave, she has her kittens. There's a box downstairs, an old banana box, and it's been the same box every year since this started. I have no idea how she knows it's our time to go, but that's when she drops. She shows us her kittens and has one last big meal. Then she takes them and heads back into the jungle, and we head back to touring, knowing we'll see her again.

JOHN MEDESKI, MUSICIAN

HUNTRESS

When my husband and I lived in a fifth-floor apartment in New York City, my Abyssinian cat, Ana Cleopatra, used to sit at the living room window and watch the birds, her teeth chattering with excitement. The window had an air conditioner in it. What we didn't realize was that the vent on one side of the air conditioner was loose. One afternoon we came home, and there was no sign of Ana. We searched the house, but no cat. Then we saw the hole next to the air conditioner, the vent pushed to one side. Our hearts sank. We thought, if Ana went after a bird and forgot she was so high up in the air, how could she survive?

We ran downstairs with heavy hearts, expecting the worst. My husband started calling her name, not even knowing where to begin looking. But as it turned out, Ana jumped from the bushes straight into his arms. She'd probably been wondering how the heck was she going to get back home. Shaken, we brought her upstairs. Miraculously, nothing was broken—she was just a little a dazed for a day or so. And then she went right back to watching the birds and chattering her teeth.

TANIA GARCIA, DESIGNER, WESTCHESTER

RIGHT:
ANONYMOUS
CAUGHT, PLACE AND DATE UNKNOWN
A solitary alley cat freezes for just a quick
moment, holding its trophy in its mouth.

FAST-N

Easy ®

CLEAR
NIA MMON

LLOWED
CHILDREN.
ck panel. .947
LITER

CAUTION: HARMFUL IF SWALLOW
IRRITANT-KEEP OUT OF REACH OF CHILD
Read carefully other cautions on back pa

TERRY DEROY GRUBER
GROCERY STORE CAT,
NEW YORK, 1979

The stock boy told me that he was over on Aisle B
with the household supplies, just stamping prices.
He reached up to a shelf and started stocking and whap!
The little monster nailed him.

I once got a scare from a little cat of ours named Charlie. I came into the kitchen and found him prostrate on his stomach on the floor, breathing heavily. In a panic, I lifted him gently and tried to get him to stand on his legs, but they collapsed under him again. And as I supported him I noticed that his stomach seemed bloated. I stood up, trying to decide whether to telephone our veterinarian or rush Charlie to the animal hospital emergency room, and then I noticed something. Almost an entire platter of spaghetti with clam sauce that had been on the counter had disappeared. Charlie wasn't suffering from some terrible neurological disorder—he'd simply OD'd on spaghetti, and his skinny adolescent legs wouldn't support his overloaded stomach.

PATRICIA CURTIS
THE INDOOR CAT

THOMAS WESTER
STOCKHOLM, SWEDEN, 1984

Moses had several homes. Unfortunately, he lived with people who turned out to be allergic to cats. He went from one foster home to another until finally, he ended up in an apartment with four girls who truly loved him. While moving from place to place, Moses learned to console himself with food and became very good at locating it. He probably weighed over fifteen pounds.

Webster was very large and very black and very composed.

He conveyed the impression of being a cat of deep reserves.

Descendant of a long line of ecclesiastical ancestors who had conducted

their decorous courtships beneath the show of cathedrals

and on the back walls of the bishops' palaces, he had that exquisite poise

which one sees in high dignitaries of the Church.

P.G. WODEHOUSE
The Story of Webster

TERRY deROY GRUBER
PARAMUS, NEW JERSEY, 1979

This seemed to me like the perfect combination. The judge holding Stanley, an Oriental
Shorthair, said, "It's tough modeling all day and traveling all over the country.
But Stanley here knows what he's doing."

WALTER CHANDOHA
You Don't Scare Me
Annandale, New Jersey, 1975

PHOTOGRAPHER UNKNOWN
Fire Department Mascot
New York, 1941

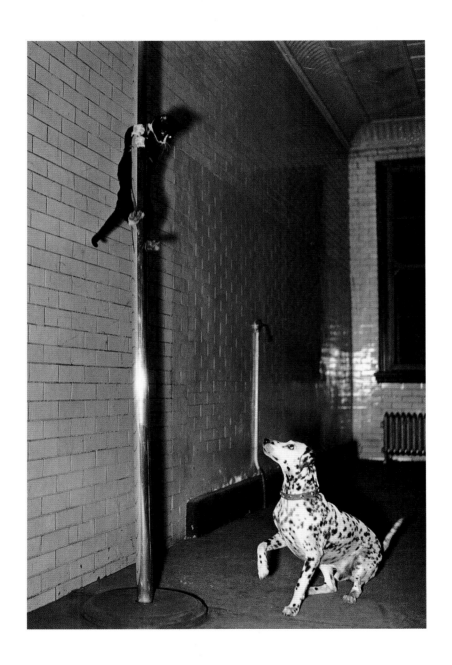

Buddies

JOHN DRYSDALE
Wild Relationship
Market Drayton,
England, 1972

Varner and Akbar are kind of cool cucumbers. I mean if there's an animal they want to hunt down and kill, they get crazed over that. I've certainly known cats that were total mushpots, but not my guys. Of course I know they love each other. They are out-and-out buddies. And I know they love us. But I couldn't quite prove it.

CONSTANCE HERNDON, EDITOR

THE ADVENTURES OF MILO AND OTIS. 1989
Above: *The American release of this Japanese film about the misadventures of Milo, a tabby kitten, and Otis, a Pug puppy, was narrated by Dudley Moore. Eighteen animal trainers worked under animal supervisor Mikio Hata on the production.*

THE WRONG BOX. 1966
Right: *In this comedy about inheritance, Peter Sellers played the mad surgeon Dr. Pratt, his office overrun by kittens. As one cat sits in the surgical bowl, the doctor contemplates the phony death certificate he's just made out for Michael Caine.*

Staying Objective

strange every time my cat
jumps on my lap to just have
some objective thought about the
cat just wanting to keep warm or
whatever. I had three cats—I lost
one in December. And my little
one, who's between five and six
years old now, has actually become
much more affectionate and enter-
taining in the past couple of
months—much more attached to
me, I think. My male cat, Ollie,
whom I've had since he was six
weeks, sleeps in my arms every
night. When I'm home he's invariably on my lap and has an incredibly loud purr. I have a recliner—
it's his chair, but he lets me sit in
it. Whenever I do, which is a lot,
he'll stand up, put his paws around
my neck, and purr into my ear. It
that a nonemotional response?

R. LEE ZASLOFF, PH.D., ASSOCIATE
DIRECTOR, CENTER FOR ANIMALS AND
SOCIETY, UNIVERSITY OF CALIFORNIA
AT DAVIS

PATRICIA MCENERY
David and Assistant
Beaulieu, France 1996

262

The Easter Cat

I always had rabbits. Then my friend's cat had kittens and I took a little white one because it looked the most like a rabbit. The kitten, Lily, grew up with rabbits hopping around. I think she knew she was not a rabbit, but she may still not know that they are not cats. As a youth Lily pulled some great capers with the bunnies—playing chase games all over the house, wrestling, nestling up to sleep with them. But she grew up to be as big as the rabbits. She could easily hurt one. Instead she guards them with great concern. If one strays into the yard, she keeps watch to make sure none of the other cats around the neighborhood mess with it. If one of the rabbits gets startled, she lies down next to it and her warmth seems to calm it down.

One time a rabbit got stuck behind the refrigerator and couldn't get out, and Lily came to my study and harassed me until I had to stop working. She leaped onto the desk and skidded into all my papers—which she knows is a bad move—and made a big racket. I finally got up and went into the kitchen to see if she was out of food. But she wasn't. Instead she led me to the refrigerator and then tried to get behind it. I thought maybe she'd lost a toy, but instead I found one of my rabbits. Or should I say our rabbits. If I hadn't have found the rabbit, it could have died.

KELLY CORE, FINANCIAL PLANNER

JOHN DRYSDALE
Peaceful Coexistence
Kings Lynn, Norfolk,
England, 1970

Overleaf:
THOMAS WESTER
Elsie Wigh
Grabo, Sweden, 1984

WALTER CHANDOHA
Of Course I Know Where I Am
Annandale, New Jersey, 1970

Beau

THOMAS WESTER
In Love
Smogen, Sweden, 1983

Until recently I had Sasha and Beau, her son. When I got Sasha she was a skinny little black cat and I had no idea she was pregnant. Actually, neither did the vet. Months later she had kittens. Beau, the gray-and-white one, stayed. He never had to leave his mother, though she wound up leaving him. Every time I came home I'd find them hugging each other on the bed, wadded together in a ball, completely a unit. Sometimes they'd spoon. When she lay down he'd walk over, lie next to her, and put his head on her lap. He was always the baby: when they were wrestling, if she got too rough on him he'd just give up and complain.

When she got sick, he freaked. That was the hardest part. He got really aggressive towards her— he'd growl when she walked towards him, as if he didn't recognize her. Maybe she smelled bad— of shots and medication. When she got too close, he'd hide under a chair. At the very end when she was really out of it, I'd bring her up on the bed for a while and when she was lying there next to me, he'd lie next to her like he used to. But I think it was because she wasn't threatening. She was still and quiet.

There were two periods of time when she was at the vet for a few days and came home again, and he was fine. But the first day she was really gone, he sat alone in the middle of the room and cried out for her like he used to as a kitten, waiting for her to call back to him. Then he seemed to realize he wasn't getting an answer, and stopped. He's eight years old now and I'm starting to see a change. He's even more demanding of attention, only now it's from me. When I'm getting ready to leave for work, he winds himself around my legs and tries to hold me up. I'm very understanding about it. We both miss his mother. I can still see her looking at me, waiting to steal my food. Beau, bless him, is entirely uninterested in food. He just wants love.

PATRICIA FABRICANT, ART DIRECTOR

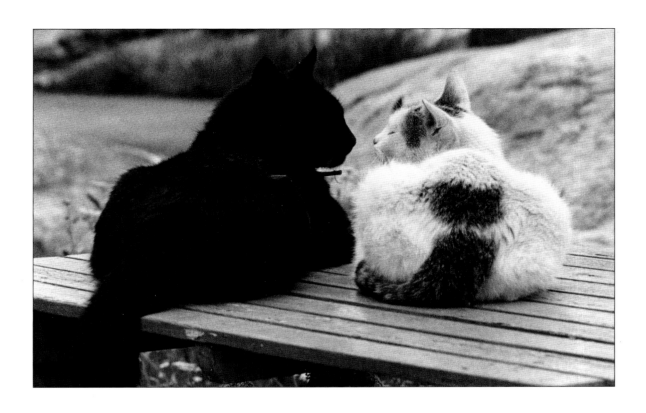

CLAUDIA GORMAN
Box Full of Fluff
Pleasant Valley, New York, 1994

I saw the most beautiful cat today. It was sitting

by the side of the road, its two front feet neatly

and graciously together. Then it gravely swished

around its tail to completely and snugly encircle

itself. It was so fit and beautifully neat, that

gesture, and so self-satisfied—so complacent.

ANNE MORROW LINDBERGH
Bring Me A Unicorn: Diaries and Letters of
Anne Morrow Lindbergh, 1922-1928

THOMAS WESTER
STOCKHOLM, SWEDEN, 1984
A formidable fat cat who weighs in at 18.5
pounds, Mose strolls the streets of southern
Stockholm with nary a care for passing cars.
Once home, he patiently waits for someone to
let him into his apartment building. Inside he
knows another good samaritan will come along
and take him up in the elevator to his floor.

Love to a Cat

KRITINA LEE KNIEF
*Muppet-Faced
Mother and Kitten
Boston, 1991*

This is how I see it: cats pretend they don't need anybody's love. This makes us feel incredibly insecure and then we lavish all this extra attention on them and then they get annoyed and reject us. Spurned like this we try even harder—special treats, extrasoft blankets, total clemency when they bring in dead birds. We decide another cat in the house might make them feel less lonely. So one day we bring in their new companion and all hell breaks loose. Our cat becomes a bully and chases the newcomer under the sofa. Our cat makes us feel awful for disrespecting her sovereignty over our house. So we feel guilty. We obsess over our latest infractions. We talk about nothing else. At the water cooler in the office, at the gym, on the phone: we confess our guilt and wonder how we will get rid of the intruder. We spend lunches finding a new home for this second-class cat. We find one and feel great—life will calm down again and our cat will be grateful for our getting rid of this problem and will become more affectionate, surely.

Then we get home to make everything nice and ready for the new owner to come for their new cat. But there is silence in the house. Both cats are hiding. See, in our absence, they have bonded. They are now inseparable. They refuse to be divided, spend every minute with each other, sleep in mirror images of each other, purr only for each other, and are united forever in their solemn pact to completely ignore us except for a perfunctory moment at mealtime. That is love, so far as I can tell, to a cat. No matter what we do, we are still left out of the picture. But actually, that's only my version. I hear of loving feline-human relationships all the time. It's just that my cats haven't.

RICHARD S., POET

JOYCE RAVID
Batty Ravid, chat de luxe
New York, 1980

MARVIN W. SCHWARTZ
Crossing the Street in the 4th
Paris, 1986
"One Sunday morning I happened to notice
this cat crossing the rue du Rosiers in the Marais.
Usually nobody notices street cats,
who are completely different from domestic ones.
They live day-to day and are the best fighters
in the world, but most of the time they're invisible.
The Marais was a very poor area before gentrification.
Now the cat lives in a housing project."

The Cure

A woman brought in a little gray kitten and said, "Rosie's listless and won't play with me." I put Rosie on the exam table and she just lay there looking pathetic, her ears hanging down. I figured she wasn't going anywhere, and left her in the room to take a phone call. But when I came back, the room was trashed. In one minute little Rosie had knocked over all the jars, scattered my papers, and shredded the happy animal posters on the wall. We found her high atop the cabinets, purring away. I told the woman, "I think she's cured."

C. KALLINI

VETERINARY ASSISTANT

TUCSON

THOMAS WESTER
Felicia's Kitten
Stockholm, Sweden, 1978

RICHARD KALVAR
PARIS, 1985

TERRY deROY GRUBER
CHINESE LAUNDRY CAT,
NEW YORK, 1979

The only thing Charlie was forbidden to do
was absolutely everything.

JIM McLAGAN
BATHTIME, 1982

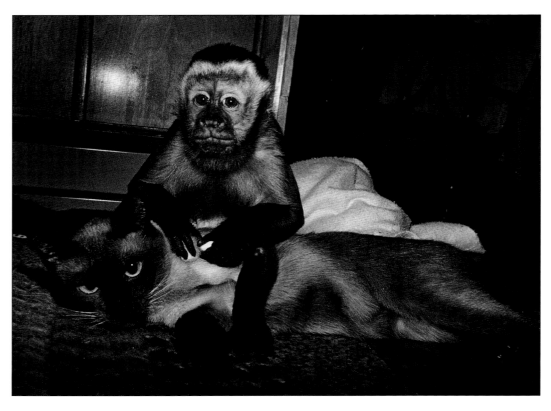

ROBIN SCHWARTZ
Teddy and Katja
Massachusetts, 1988

JOHN DRYSDALE
Tom and Jerry Sharing
Kings Lynn, Norfolk,
England, 1970

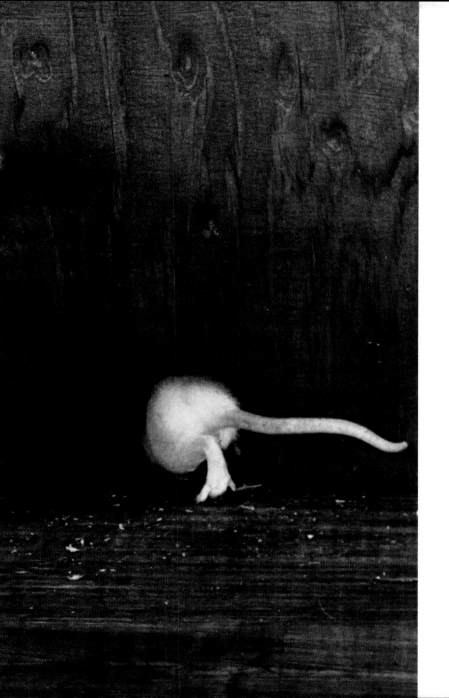

PHOTOGRAPHER UNKNOWN
"Farewell," from the "Hail,
Quail, and Farewell" Series
Coral Gables, Florida, c. 1947

Actress Yvonne De Carlo, known for her role as
Lily on *The Munsters*, with a beautiful fat Persian.

A home without a cat and

a well-fed, well-petted

and properly revered

cat, may be a perfect

home, perhaps, but how

can it prove its title?

MARK TWAIN

THOMAS WESTER
RAMKVILLA, SWEDEN, 1984
"I met this farm woman, Maria, when I was hiking in
the woods of Småland. She obliged me by allowing
me to photograph her seventeen-pound cat."

Even overweight cats instinctively

know the cardinal rule: when

fat, arrange yourself in slim poses.

JOHN WITY
Cat Quotations

CHAIM KANNER
VENICE, ITALY, 1987

"This cat acted like a dog out for a stroll with his
master. He was placid, complacent, and unafraid."

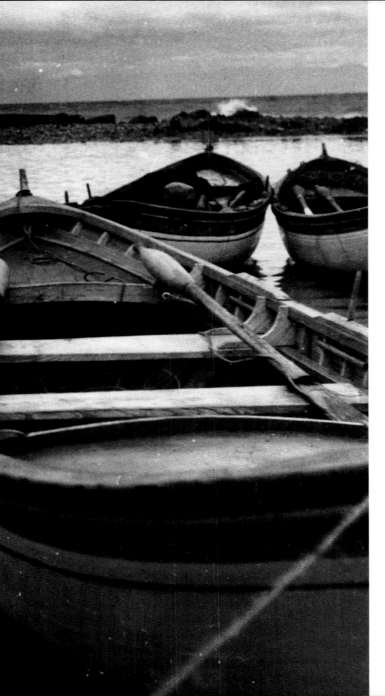

**ANONYMOUS
DOCK CAT,
NEW ENGLAND**

As familiar with boats and water as he is
with land, a burly fisherman's cat transverses
the rowboats on his way in for the night.

OVERLEAF:
**UPI PHOTOGRAPHER
SWIMMER THE KITTEN,
SANTA MONICA,
CALIFORNIA, 1956**

Ten-year-old Donna Pick helped her two-
and-a-half-month-old tabby kitten get used
to the water by pulling her on a raft. Soon
the cat was leaping off a diving board
and coming along for morning laps.

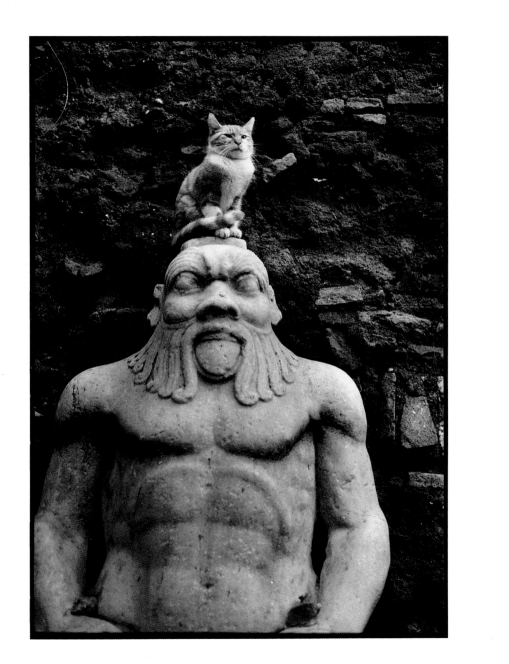

ELLIOTT ERWITT
ROME, ITALY, 1959

LIZZIE HIMMEL
The Turkish Cat
Istanbul, Turkey, 1989
"He seemed very young but he also clearly owned the house:
though I played with him a lot, I couldn't get him to leave the doorway.
As usual, I was on vacation so I could take pictures of cats—
my reason, always, for going to another city."

Opposite:
EUGENE ATGÉT
Coeur de Rouen
1915

TONY MENDOZA
NEW YORK, NY, 1993

"This big white cat belonged to a neighbor.
I simply call him New York City cat."

RIGHT:

ELLIOTT ERWITT
PLACE UNKNOWN, 1975

"I don't always remember where I took a photograph.
I just take the picture and then forget about it. This is just
a cat lying on a patio table, but what a cat!"

OVERLEAF:

THOMAS WESTER
STOCKHOLM, SWEDEN, 1984

After a 621-mile flight to be mated,
this sly little puss changed her mind.

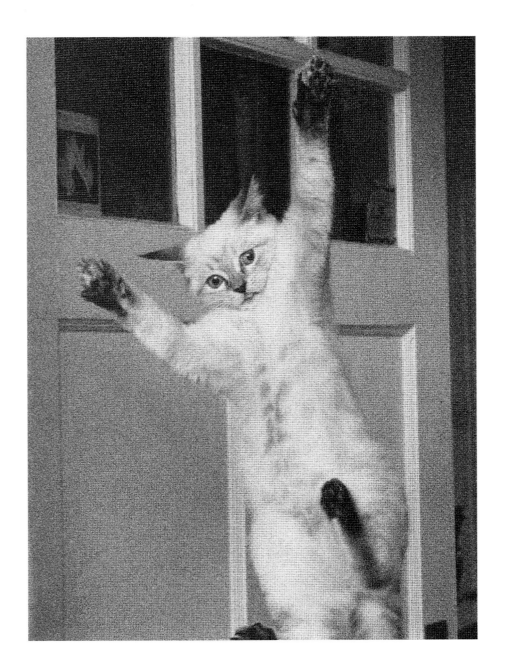

WALTER CHANDOHA
Tudor City Cat
New York, 1970
"In those days, the East Side had a lot of character.
The cat, for instance—he was clearly from the neighborhood—
didn't budge an inch when I poked my camera in his face."

The Profound Feline

To think that cats don't have wonderful feelings is human arrogance. We're mammals, cats are mammals; we all have these feelings because we are mammals, not because we are people. And think of it: love has powerful evolutionary value—for those whose system requires them to keep together and cooperate, positive feelings for each other will make life go so much more smoothly. In our culture, we put tremendous importance on romantic love. But friendship-based love can be very strong—the love between siblings, parent and child, companions. Even in long-standing couples, that's the glue that holds us together—and cats too. One kind of love is more stormy, the other is more profound. Perhaps we could say that cats are more profound.

ELIZABETH MARSHALL THOMAS,
ANTHROPOLOGIST AND AUTHOR

JOHN DRYSDALE
Kitten with
Powerful Friendship
Welwyn Garden City,
England, 1979

Previous pages:
DAVID MCENERY
Catville Tours,
Santa Monica Beach, 1994
"There was a guy on the
Santa Monica Beach for a
while who lived in a bus,
and travelled with some
twenty-five cats. They were
very accustomed to bus life."

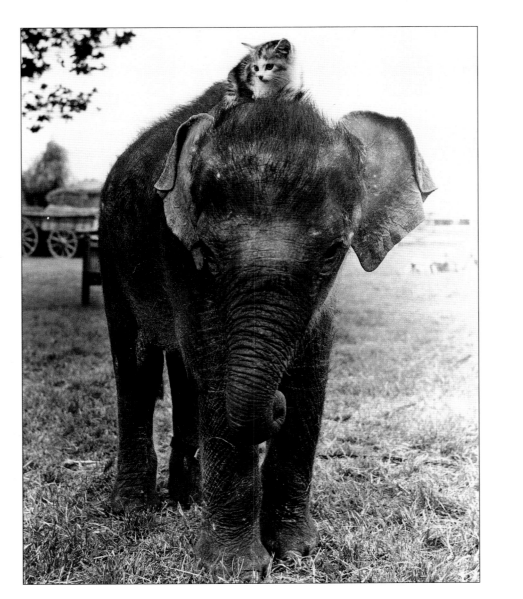

ARIES (March 21—April 20)

The original cat on a hot tin roof, most active and ambitious of them all. From clean laundry to flower beds, he makes a (hollow) impression everywhere. Fond of wandering, and when at home liable to create his own obstacle course with no inhibitions about broken ornaments.

Fond of fighting, impetuous at loving.

Best Owners (only owners able to survive him): Sagittarius, Leo.

ANN CURRAH
The Cat Horoscope

PHOTOGRAPHER UNKNOWN
AUDREY HEPBURN AND THE CAT CALLED CAT, 1961

Orangey, a 14-pound prima donna, is a legend in the small world of feline acting. His Patsy-award winning performance in Breakfast at Tiffany's required all the efforts of his trainer, Frank Inn, including guard dogs at the exits so Orangey would stick around. It was his second Patsy, the first gleaned from his work in the 1952 feature Rhubarb, which also earned him the title, "The World's Meanest Cat."

BREAKFAST AT TIFFANY'S, 1961
Above and left: *Defining cat irascibility for all movies to come,*
Orangey method-acted his way through the Audrey Hepburn-
George Peppard romance in trademark style. As "Cat," Holly
Golightly's "poor slob without a name," Orangey jumped onto
the back of his hungover mistress to wake her up, and then
leaped from the floor to Peppard's shoulders to a nearby shelf.

A cat I keep

that lays about my house

Grown fat with eating

Many a miching mouse.

ROBERT HERRICK

BREAKFAST AT TIFFANY'S. 1961
Above and left: *Defining cat irascibility for all movies to come,
Orangey method-acted his way through the Audrey Hepburn-
George Peppard romance in trademark style. As "Cat," Holly
Golightly's "poor slob without a name," Orangey jumped onto
the back of his hungover mistress to wake her up, and then
leaped from the floor to Peppard's shoulders to a nearby shelf.*

That Barn Cat

JOHN DRYSDALE
Kitten Makes an Ass of Itself
Glamorgan, Wales, 1981

There's a cat in love with my horse Harpo these days. The cat is a big old barn tom, but Harpo's a Thoroughbred, and was pretty high-strung until the cat came around. In the morning when I go to feed him that cat is always lying in the feed bin. If Harpo lies down for a nap, the cat lies down between his front legs, and Harpo is very careful not to move them. They play hide-and-seek out in the field: Harpo nickers and lowers his nose to the grass and the cat meows and pounces. Thing is, this cat doesn't give a hoot about any other animals—not the dog or the other cats, or even the other horses. Harpo is it. And if I go for a ride, I can lift the cat up with me and he'll stay on the whole way. I hold the cat and the cat holds Harpo, holding onto the mane with his teeth.

ANNE FORELLI, RESEARCH BIOLOGIST

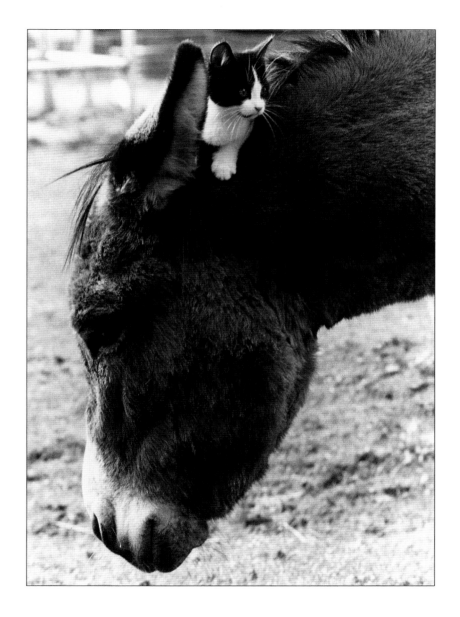

A cat I keep

that lays about my house

Grown fat with eating

Many a miching mouse.

ROBERT HERRICK

RIGHT:
THOMAS WESTER
KALMAR, SWEDEN, 1977

"This cat, Felicia, or Puppan in Swedish, had
eaten her Christmas rice pudding and then
settled in for a long snooze near the warm
radiator. She weighs about thirteen pounds."

OVERLEAF:
THOMAS WESTER
STOCKHOLM, SWEDEN, 1990

"This fat cat loves to take sunbaths."

Grinch and the Burmese

WALTER CHANDOHA
City Courtship on 46th Street
New York, 1950

The animal clinic I work in got in a burly cat that was part Persian and all grump. A tooth infection made him so irritable he hated to be touched—though his owner said that was nothing new. His nickname was Grinch. After surgery I put him in the cat room in a quiet cage next to a little Burmese that ignored everyone. She was a sad little cat: her owner was away on business a lot, and the cat boarded here. It didn't seem like much of a life.

When I went to check on Grinch's recovery I thought, "Well, he'll probably be in a really bad mood." I shoved my hands into my pockets to keep myself from reflexively reaching for him and getting clawed, and walked into the cat room. There was Grinch, sitting up with his eyes shut, purring so loudly the cage rattled. His lips were curled into a funny smile and his tongue was hanging out. His paws did little kneading motions into the blanket.

I was really worried. Did I have a stoned cat on my hands? Had I given him too much anesthetic? I checked the dosage, but it was right. Then I noticed the little Burmese—she was kind of hidden, crouching right next to him. She was grooming him through the bars. This was the source of Grinch's bliss. He lay down like a majestic lion and the Burmese followed, pressing herself closely against him. They turned their heads towards each other as if they were lovers inhaling each other's wonderful scents. They slept all day like that.

The next morning, when Grinch's owner came to get him, he hissed at her. He yowled from his crate and the Burmese yowled back. It was cacaphony. None of us knew what to do. Home, he hid from his owner and scratched up the furniture. And the Burmese, here, went on a hunger strike.

But this story has a happy ending. Grinch's owner, desperate to have a mellower cat, offered to take the Burmese. The Burmese's owner agreed to let her cat go live with Grinch. Now Grinch has no more tantrums, and the Burmese is sleek and fat. If one has to go to the vet, they come together. The Burmese needed to stay overnight recently and Grinch stayed with her. They were in heaven. It was like a second honeymoon.

CHRISTOPHER KALLINI,
VETERINARY ASSISTANT

Grinch and the Burmese

WALTER CHANDOHA
City Courtship on 46th Street
New York, 1950

The animal clinic I work in got in a burly cat that was part Persian and all grump. A tooth infection made him so irritable he hated to be touched—though his owner said that was nothing new. His nickname was Grinch. After surgery I put him in the cat room in a quiet cage next to a little Burmese that ignored everyone. She was a sad little cat: her owner was away on business a lot, and the cat boarded here. It didn't seem like much of a life.

When I went to check on Grinch's recovery I thought, "Well, he'll probably be in a really bad mood." I shoved my hands into my pockets to keep myself from reflexively reaching for him and getting clawed, and walked into the cat room. There was Grinch, sitting up with his eyes shut, purring so loudly the cage rattled. His lips were curled into a funny smile and his tongue was hanging out. His paws did little kneading motions into the blanket.

I was really worried. Did I have a stoned cat on my hands? Had I given him too much anesthetic? I checked the dosage, but it was right. Then I noticed the little Burmese—she was kind of hidden, crouching right next to him. She was grooming him through the bars. This was the source of Grinch's bliss. He lay down like a majestic lion and the Burmese followed, pressing herself closely against him. They turned their heads towards each other as if they were lovers inhaling each other's wonderful scents. They slept all day like that.

The next morning, when Grinch's owner came to get him, he hissed at her. He yowled from his crate and the Burmese yowled back. It was cacaphony. None of us knew what to do. Home, he hid from his owner and scratched up the furniture. And the Burmese, here, went on a hunger strike.

But this story has a happy ending. Grinch's owner, desperate to have a mellower cat, offered to take the Burmese. The Burmese's owner agreed to let her cat go live with Grinch. Now Grinch has no more tantrums, and the Burmese is sleek and fat. If one has to go to the vet, they come together. The Burmese needed to stay overnight recently and Grinch stayed with her. They were in heaven. It was like a second honeymoon.

CHRISTOPHER KALLINI,
VETERINARY ASSISTANT

RIGHT:

ROBIN SCHWARTZ
NEW YORK, NY, 1994

"This fat cat belongs to the owners of the
Pet Bar in Greenwich Village. He was tethered on a
leash but seemed to be enjoying himself."

DAVID McENERY
Life of Reilly
Santa Monica, California, 1992

overleaf:
YLLA
Six Siamese Kittens
New York City, c. 1950

Don Gato of W. 105th Street

MARY BLOOM
Meri and Kitten
Sharon, Connecticut, 1983

When I lived in Spanish Harlem, I had a cat who was clearly in love with my girlfriend. Even after we got him fixed, he'd get all aroused. Every night he would come into bed and move against her. He was definitely a passionate cat. One day he was resting on the windowsill and it started to rain. I was asleep under the window. In a half-conscious state I reached up to close it and instead of coming in the cat jumped out—three flights down. He wound up hanging around in the backyard having a quick fling with a girl cat, and then came back up three days later, completely unhurt. He was hungry, but he was happy. And he stopped bothering my girlfriend.

BEN PEROWSKI, DRUMMER

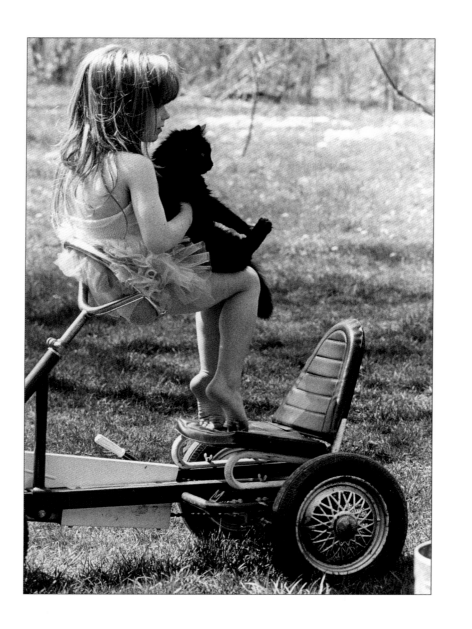

KRITINA LEE KNIEF
Captain, Spaghetti and Cat
Venice, 1992

As anyone who has ever been around

a cat for any length of time well knows,

cats have enormous patience with the

limitations of the human mind.

CLEVELAND AMORY
The Quotable Feline

RIGHT:
THOMAS WESTER
SUNDRE, GOTLAND, SWEDEN, 1985
This fat cat weighs in at 15.4 pounds and
loves to amuse himself in the dining room.

OVERLEAF:
KARL BADEN
CAMBRIDGE, MA, 1990
"Ohmie has belonged to a friend for eighteen years. On a
visit to the local animal hospital, despite her girth, the vet,
amazed at what great shape she was in for a cat of her
age, said, 'This cat has the body of a twelve-year-old.'"

ROBIN SCHWARTZ
NOAH, 1993

That's my boy, a Cornish Rex, at five. He's extremely attached and personable.
The thing about Rexes is that they act like dogs. People say that I have a dog that acts like a cat
and cats that act like dogs. Noah stands at the top of the shower doors when I take a shower and
sleeps in the baby bed when I work. Here he has the night crazies and is just trying to be funny.

KARL BADEN
CAT SHOW, BOXBOROUGH, MASSACHUSETTS, 1993

I often find the cages as interesting as the cats.

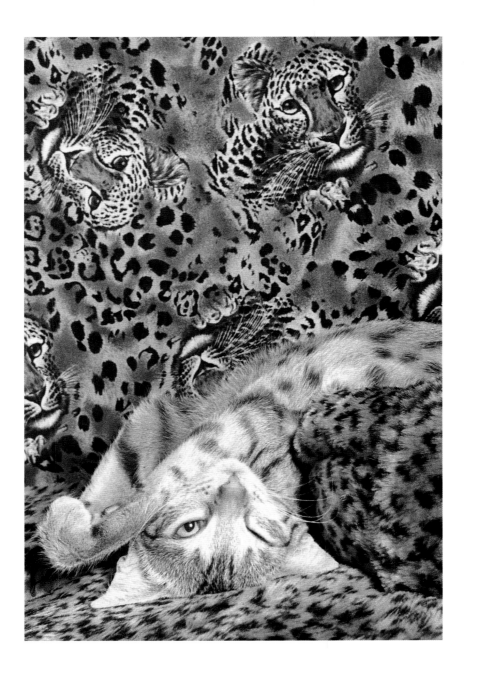

LARS PETER ROOS
CATNAP,
WEST AFRICA, 1986

"My friend was working on a health project in West Africa, and I was her houseguest. Her kitten, a little tabby, followed me everywhere. He had the habit of figuring out just where I wanted to be and getting right in that spot. Or lying on the piece of paper I was writing on until he lost interest and fell asleep."

350

YLLA
Diable and Goldfish
New York City, c. 1950

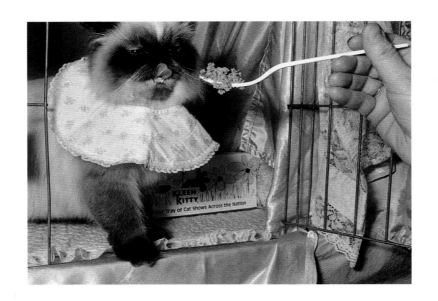

ABOVE:

KARL BADEN

CAT AND FORK, BOSTON, 1992

"You'd think that this cat wore a bib for mealtime.
Actually a lot of long-haired cats wear bibs at cat
shows, so they won't lick themselves and mess
up their hair before they're judged."

RIGHT:

ROBIN SCHWARTZ

CHANEL, NEW YORK CITY, 1996

"This lion-cut calico Persian named Chanel is a veteran
show cat. She comes to Madison Square Garden every
year from Florida, where she lives with Lise, her owner,
who's a groomer. Chanel is thirteen years old. I think
older cats have more of a sense of laissez-faire than
younger ones. They have a certain dignity about them
that comes from having been around the block."

ROBIN SCHWARTZ
NEW YORK, NY, 1994

"A Norwegian Forest cat at the
International Cat Show in
Madison Square Garden.
His name is Billy Joe."

BELL, BOOK AND CANDLE. 1958
A feline-eyed Kim Novak holds Pyewacket the Siamese as she brews up a witch's plot to win James Stewart's love. The cat won a Patsy Award—the American Humane Association's Picture Animal Top Star of the Year award—for his performance.

BELL, BOOK AND CANDLE. 1958
*James Stewart looks with amazement at Kim Novak's feline
ally, Pyewacket, who is asleep in the witch's arms.*

CAT PEOPLE. 1942
*Jane Randolph comforts the kitten that's been mewing away in
a box all day. Presented by Kent Smith to his mysterious
girlfriend, Simone Simon, the kitten hissed with terror and had
to be taken away—the first hint that Simon had an uneasy
connection with the feline world. Brought to the office, the cat
does fine with thoroughly human Randolph.*

ABOVE AND RIGHT:

DONNA RUSKIN
SEBASTIAN ON THE SINK,
SEBASTIAN IN THE SINK,
YONKERS, NEW YORK, 1988

"I know some cats like to stay cool in the summer, but this was in October, and it wasn't particularly hot at all. Sebastian just likes cool, smooth places. Maybe he's trying to say something about his personality. Actually, he's not that smooth, he's just very present. This was taken in the morning: I was starting to brush my teeth, and he just wanted to be where I needed to be. In a minute, he probably started talking, because he's also very vocal. I have a friend who wants to make a video of him talking. He's sure we could win a big prize on *America's Funniest Home Videos*."

THE BLUE BIRD. 1976
This tuxedo-patterned Domestic American Longhair starred in
20th Century Fox's remake of this children's tale filmed in
Moscow. Elizabeth Taylor, Cicely Tyson, and Jane Fonda were
among the other stars in the lavish fantasy.

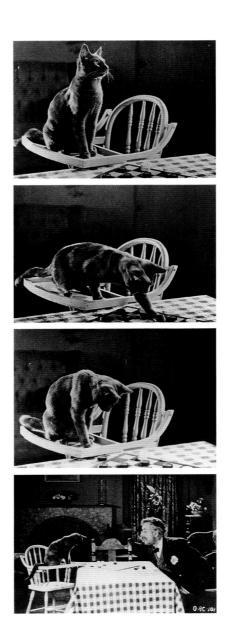

PEPPER THE CAT. 1920S

The gray cat climbed up through a broken floorboard and right into Mack Sennett's Hollywood studio, where she was immediately installed in the scene being shot. She performed beautifully. Sennett christened her Pepper and made her the feline star of many silents. Her curiosity made her a fast learner. She picked up checkers instantly to play with comedian Ben Turpin, and formed a lasting partnership with Teddy, the Sennett studio's Great Dane. In mourning for the departed dog, she ended her career just as she'd started it— by refusing to stay on the set.

ROBIN SCHWARTZ
BALOO, NEW YORK, 1993

Baloo was at the Madison Square Garden Cat Show in March. She's a Norwegian Forest Cat. She was just hanging out on the chair, very laid back. I think it's remarkable for a cat to act that way at a cat show. I'd be a wreck if I were a cat at a cat show.

TWO OF A KIND

My friend who's extremely plump has a cat who out of sympathy became quite large as well, until the two of them were just enormous. The cat, though, is very proud of his bulk and carries it quite well, while his owner, on the other hand, seems quite embarrassed for himself.

**VIVIEN GOLDMAN, MUSIC WRITER,
NEW YORK AND LONDON**

RIGHT:
**MARJORIE LUNDEN
I'M READY, STOCKHOLM, 1996**
"When you point a camera at my cat, he poses. Cats are
much more aware than we think they are. How else do
you explain a cat who walks into a photographer's house
and becomes her best model, always aware of the lens?"

OVERLEAF:
**PALMER M. PEDERSEN
FOLLOW ME, MONTANA, 1955**
Neighboring rancher and amateur photographer Palmer
Pedersen caught this seven-member procession walking
along the crest of a Montana hill. Like kittens following
their mother, these cats stay close to their elderly owner.

Page 1:
WALTER CHANDOHA
Toughie
Hunterdon County, New Jersey, 1969

Page 2:
WALTER CHANDOHA
Follow Me
Long Island, New York, 1967

Page 4:
JAN RIETZ
Looking for Food
Skane, Sweden, 1995

Pages 8-9:
DAVID MCENERY
Blackjack
Redondo Beach, California, 1994

PHOTOGRAPHY CREDITS

Walter Chandoha: Pages 1, 3, 17, 25, 26, 28-9, 36-7, 39, 43, 49, 55, 69, 75, 76-7, 80, 81, 83, 218-9, 221, 254-5, 269, 271, 317, 333
© Jan Rietz/Tiofoto AB: Pages 4, 21
© David McEnery: Pages 8-9, 12-13, 31, 45, 65, 70-1, 105, 119, 156-7, 172, 195, 216-7, 223, 318-9, 336-7
© Claudia Gorman: Pages 11, 273, 315
© Studio Lemaire/Art Unlimited, Amsterdam: Page 15
© Marilaide Ghigliano: Page 18
© Guy le Querrec/Magnum Photos: Page 23
© Express Newspapers/Archive Photos: Page 27
© Donna Ruskin: Pages 32-3, 134, 143, 366, 367

Courtesy UPI/Corbis-Bettmann: Pages 34, 67, 99, 100-1, 203, 205, 302-3, 304-5, 380-1
© Johan Willner/Tiofoto AB: Page 35
Ylla, © Pryor Dodge: Pages 40, 127, 338-9, 352-3
© Lambert/Archive Photos: Pages 41, 73
Courtesy R. P. Kingston: Pages 42, 185
© Karl Baden: Pages 46-7, 120, 346-7, 349, 354, 365
© Nick Nichols/Magnum Photos: Page 51
Courtesy Express Newspapers/Archive Photos: Pages 52-3
© Thomas Wester: Pages 56, 60-1, 87, 95, 96-7, 102, 103, 116-7, 146-7, 155, 163, 175, 183, 199, 207, 235, 251, 266-7, 275, 283, 299, 312-3, 329, 330-1, 345
© Laura Straus: Page 59
© Andrea Mohin: Page 63
© Michael Nichols/Magnum Photos: Page 64
© Jayne Hinds Bidaut: Page 79
© Archive Photos: Pages 84-5
Courtesy Archive Photos: Pages 88, 89, 149, 151, 193, 196-7, 200, 201, 227, 229, 236-7, 297, 371
Courtesy Bettman/UPI: Pages 91, 132, 133, 220, 257, 287
© John Drysdale: Pages 92-3, 114-5, 179, 259, 265, 293, 321, 327
© Terry deRoy Gruber: Pages 106-7, 130-1, 176-7, 248-9, 253, 288-9, 362-3
© Per Wichmann: Pages 108-9, 110-1, 245
© Robin Schwartz: Pages 112, 113, 122, 123, 125, 136-7, 139, 145, 158-9, 160-1, 186-7, 191, 292, 335, 348, 355, 356-7
© Ann Finnell: Pages 121, 180-1, 230-1, 377
© Kritina Lee Knief: Pages 128-9, 144, 148, 165, 167, 171, 173, 277, 343
© Mikael Bertmar/Tiofoto AB: Page 135

DO CATS DREAM?

Published in 2004 by Welcome Books®
An imprint of Welcome Enterprises, Inc.
6 West 18th Street
New York, NY 10011
(212) 989-3200; Fax (212) 989-3205
www.welcomebooks.biz

Publisher: Lena Tabori
Project Director: Alice Wong
Designer: J.C. Suarès
Project Assistant: Larry Chesler

Distributed to the trade in the U.S. and Canada by
Andrews McMeel Distribution Services
Order Department and Customer Service: (800) 943-9839
Orders-only Fax: (800) 943-9831

The publishers gratefully acknowledge the permission of
the following to reprint the copyrighted material in this
book:

Excerpt on pg. 20: Translated by Patrick and Justina
Gregory, in *The Fables of Aesop*, selected and illustrated by
David Levine, © 1975, David Levine.

Excerpt on pg. 22 from "the song of mehitabel" from *archy
and mehitabel*, by Don Marquis, © 1927 by Doubleday, a
division of Bantam Doubleday Dell Publishing Group, Inc.
Reprinted by permission of the publisher.

Excerpt on pg. 138 from "How the Cat Became," in *How
the Whale Became and Other Stories*, by Ted Hughes, © Ted
Hughes, 1963, Faber and Faber Ltd., publishers.

Excerpts on pp. 151, 252: P.G. Wodehouse, "The Story
of Webster," permission given by A.P. Watt on behalf of
the Trustees of the Wodehouse Estate.

Excerpt on pg. 226: *The Papers of Samuel Marchbanks*, ©
1986 by Robertson Davies. Used by permission of Viking
Penguin, a division of Penguin Books, USA, Inc.

Excerpt on pg. 250: *The Indoor Cat*, © 1981 by Patricia
Curtis. Reprinted by permission of Doubleday, a division
of Bantam Doubleday Dell Publishing Group, Inc.

Excerpt on pg. 274: *Bring Me A Unicorn: Diaries and Letters
of Anne Morrow Lindbergh, 1922-1928,* © 1972 by Anne
Morrow Lindbergh. Reprinted by permission of Harcourt,
Brace & Company.

Every attempt has been made to obtain permission to
reproduce materials protected by copyright. Where
omissions may have occurred, the publisher will be happy
to acknowledge this in future printings.

Library of Congress Cataloging-in-Publication Data on file.

ISBN 1-932183-20-5

Printed in Singapore

First Edition

10 9 8 7 6 5 4 3 2 1